W9-BFS-880

GEOTECHNICAL ENGINEERING
AND Earth's Materials and Processes

Crabtree Publishing Company
www.crabtreebooks.com

Rebecca Sjonger

Crabtree Publishing Company

www.crabtreebooks.com

Author: Rebecca Sjonger

**Publishing plan research
and development:** Reagan Miller

Photo research: James Nixon

Editors: Paul Humphrey, James Nixon,
Kathy Middleton

Consultant: Carolyn De Cristofano, M.Ed.
STEM consultant, Professional Development Director
of Engineering is Elementary (2005-2008)

Proofreader: Wendy Scavuzzo

Layout: sprout.uk.com

Cover design and logo: Margaret Amy Salter

**Production coordinator and prepress
technician:** Margaret Amy Salter

Print coordinator: Margaret Amy Salter

Written and produced for Crabtree Publishing Company
by Discovery Books

Photographs:
Alamy: pp. 4 (qaphotos.com), 16 (qaphotos.com), 17
(qaphotos.com), 22 (Sarah Quill).
Bigstock: pp. 6 (Lakeview Images), 8 top (Pixart), 8
bottom (designua), 9 (Tomato), 11 top (ironrodart), 11
bottom (Daniel Prudek), 12 (Ocean and Design), 13
top (Darrenp), 13 bottom (pauldclarke), 14 (darios), 15
top (Vitaliy Pakhnyushchyy), 19 (Photo.ua), 20 bottom
(yampi), 21 (AdMeskens), 28 (marczes), 29 bottom
(bloodua).
Getty Images: pp. 11 middle (Kevin Schafer), 18 (Key-
stone-France), 20 top (Jose Luis Pelaez Inc), 24 (Marco
Secchi), 25 (Melanie Stetson Freeman/The Christian
Science Monitor), 26 (David M. Levitt/Bloomberg), 29
top (NASSER YOUNES/AFP).
Science Photo Library: p. 23 (VOLKER STEGER).
Shutterstock: Cover (all images), p. 5 (Rook76).
Wikimedia: p. 15 bottom (Los Angeles Public Library).

Library and Archives Canada Cataloguing in Publication

Sjonger, Rebecca, author
Geotechnical engineering and Earth's materials and processes
/ Rebecca Sjonger.

(Engineering in action)
Includes index.
Issued in print and electronic formats.
ISBN 978-0-7787-7506-5 (bound).--
ISBN 978-0-7787-7534-8 (paperback).--
ISBN 978-1-4271-9998-0 (pdf).--ISBN 978-1-4271-9994-2 (html)

1. Geotechnical engineering--Juvenile literature. I. Title. II.
Series: Engineering in action (St. Catharines, Ont.)

TA705.S56 2015   j624.1'51   C2015-903393-4
C2015-903394-2

Library of Congress Cataloging-in-Publication Data

Sjonger, Rebecca, author.
Geotechnical engineering and Earth's materials and processes /
Rebecca Sjonger.
pages cm. -- (Engineering in action)
Includes index.
ISBN 978-0-7787-7506-5 (reinforced library binding) --
ISBN 978-0-7787-7534-8 (pbk.) --
ISBN 978-1-4271-9998-0 (electronic pdf) --
ISBN 978-1-4271-9994-2 (electronic html)
1. Geotechnical engineering--Juvenile literature. 2. Soil mechanics--
Juvenile literature. I. Title. II. Series: Engineering in action.
TA705.S5384 2016
624.1'51--dc23

2015020443

Crabtree Publishing Company

www.crabtreebooks.com   1-800-387-7650

Printed in the USA/012016/CG20151208

**Published in Canada
Crabtree Publishing**
616 Welland Ave.
St. Catharines, ON
L2M 5V6

**Published in the United States
Crabtree Publishing**
PMB 59051
350 Fifth Avenue, 59th Floor
New York, New York 10118

**Published in the United Kingdom
Crabtree Publishing**
Maritime House
Basin Road North, Hove
BN41 1WR

**Published in Australia
Crabtree Publishing**
3 Charles Street
Coburg North
VIC, 3058

CONTENTS

What is geotechnical engineering?   4

Minerals and rocks   6

Soil   8

Forces and stresses   10

Natural hazards   12

Building on the past   14

Modern geotechnical engineers   16

Starting the process   18

Searching for solutions   20

Prototype testing cycle   22

Sharing the results   24

Design challenge   26

Into the future   28

Learning more   30

Glossary   31

Index   32

WHAT IS GEOTECHNICAL ENGINEERING?

What do skyscrapers, bridges, and tunnels have in common? Rocks and soil support them all. Earth's materials are beneath everything from homes to **landfills**. Geotechnical engineers sample, study, and test these materials. They design **foundations** and supports to suit the ground conditions. They consider the natural processes that affect new and developed sites. Their work helps make buildings stable and safe for the people who use them.

Engineering and science: Many closely related science and engineering fields focus on Earth's materials and processes. Each field has a different goal. For example, geologists are scientists who want to discover as much as they can about how Earth and its materials formed. Geotechnical engineers also investigate Earth's materials. However, they apply what they learn and find practical solutions. For example, when they study soil, it is so their designs work with the properties of that soil. These properties include soil texture, how it holds water, and how it compacts, or joins together, under pressure. Geoenvironmental engineers specialize in solving environmental problems created by people's use of Earth's materials. One area of focus for these engineers is improving polluted soil.

To create strong foundations, geotechnical engineers include materials such as steel bars in their designs.

4

Eight steps to success: Geotechnical engineers follow a series of steps to design, build, and test solutions, such as innovative foundations. The process for creating strong, safe designs is as follows:

KARL VON TERZAGHI

The Massachusetts Institute of Technology (MIT) in the United States built on a new site in 1916. Within a few years, it faced a big problem. The new buildings were sinking into the soil. John Freeman was one of the lead engineers working with MIT. He knew exactly whose help they needed. Austrian Karl von Terzaghi had written the first book about **soil mechanics** in 1924. It described what happens to soil under different conditions. MIT offered von Terzaghi a one-year teaching job in the United States. They hoped that he could also explain why their school buildings were sinking. The professor stayed for an extra three years and advised MIT on its soil issues. During that time, soil mechanics gained attention around the world. It marked the beginning of the modern field of geotechnical engineering.

Karl von Terzaghi studied mechanical and structural engineering before focusing on soil mechanics.

Steps in the design process

Define the problem

↓

Identify criteria and constraints

↓

Brainstorm ideas

↓

Select a solution

↓

Build a prototype

Improve the design   Test the prototype

↓

Communicate the solution

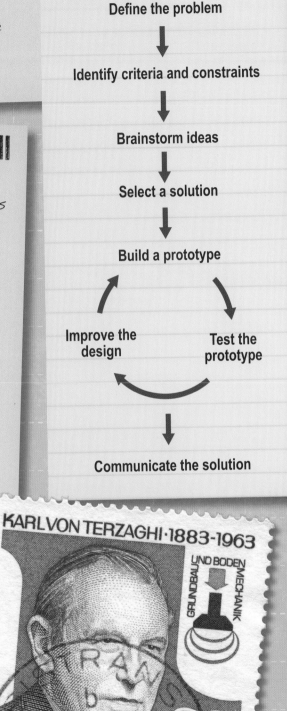

KARL VON TERZAGHI · 1883–1963

GRUNDBAU UND BODENMECHANIK

S3

REPUBLIK ÖSTERREICH
1983

MINERALS AND ROCKS

Geotechnical engineers study **minerals**, rocks, and soil so they can design strong, safe foundations. Minerals are the main substances in rock and soil. For example, sandy soil and rock called granite often contain the mineral quartz. Minerals, rocks, and soil are the materials that make up Earth's outer layer, called the crust. The crust covers the mantle—a dense layer of minerals and rocks. Where these layers meet, heavy rocks push against each other and intense pressure builds. The extreme heat and pressure slowly change solid minerals and rocks trapped in this boundary into liquid **magma**. Look at the rock cycle diagram opposite. Can you see why heat, pressure, and magma are important to rock formation?

Core samples: Geotechnical engineers study and test the rocks and bedrock found at new and existing building sites. Bedrock is the solid layer that lies beneath the soil. It may be shallow or very deep. Engineers drill into the rock with hollow tubes that pull out **core samples**. The samples give them a lot of information, such as the minerals the bedrock contains. Knowing what the bedrock is made up of helps with planning foundations and structures. Engineers also test core samples for strength. Labs have technologies and equipment that put increasing amounts of pressure on solid rock samples until they break. This shows what forces the rock can bear, which is important to know before starting the design process.

These tubes contain core samples of rock that will go to a lab for testing.

THE ROCK CYCLE

1 Heat and pressure cause underground metamorphic rock to melt. It becomes magma. When magma cools, it hardens into igneous rock.

2 Underground temperatures and pressure that are not high enough to create magma can cause igneous rock to change into a new solid form called metamorphic rock.

3 Over time, agents such as wind and water break down metamorphic rock on Earth's surface. Sedimentary rock forms when pieces of metamorphic rock, and sometimes materials such as broken shells, compact under pressure and cement together.

4 Hot temperatures and pressure cause underground sedimentary rock to change form and become metamorphic rock.

5 Underground sedimentary rock becomes magma due to very intense heat and pressure. When the magma cools and hardens, it becomes igneous rock.

There are three main kinds of rock: *igneous*, *metamorphic*, and *sedimentary*. They are always moving through the rock cycle. These changes can take a long time—even millions of years. The numbers in the diagram are different ways in which a type of rock may change to another type.

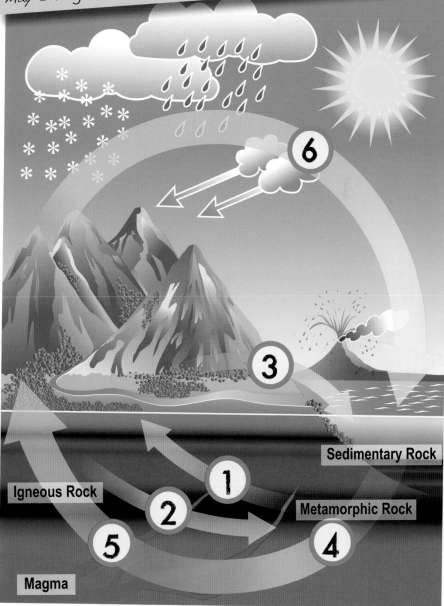

Sedimentary Rock

Igneous Rock

Metamorphic Rock

Magma

6 Agents such as wind and water cause pieces of igneous rock to break away and become **sediment**. This cements and compacts into sedimentary rock.

SOIL

Natural processes break and wear down rocks, which helps create soil. Weathering is a natural process that occurs when freezing, thawing, and weather conditions affect rocks. Another form of weathering

Over millions of years, weathering and erosion shape soft sedimentary rock into these formations, called hoodoos.

occurs when rocks crumble because of growing plant roots or animal activity. Human activities can increase weathering. For example, **acid rain** caused by pollution slowly dissolves rocks. After weathering takes place, **erosion** is the process that carries away sediment. It travels on water, wind, and ice floes. Fine pieces of sediment become soil.

Soil basics: Soil contains water and air and broken-down rocks. Dead plants and animals that have **decomposed** are also part of soil. Different mixtures of natural materials create different soils. Climate also affects how soil forms. For example, sandy deserts develop in very dry climates. The main types of soil that geotechnical engineers work with are **clay**, sand, and **silt**. Each type contains different materials and has grains that are different sizes and shapes. Two layers of soil sit above bedrock. The upper layer is called topsoil. It contains the air, water, and minerals that plants need to grow. Subsoil is a denser lower layer that holds more water.

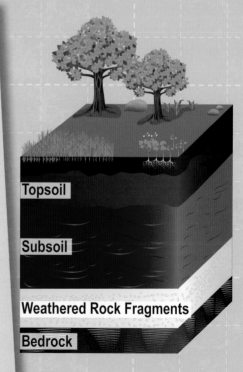

Topsoil

Subsoil

Weathered Rock Fragments

Bedrock

The cross-section of topsoil, subsoil, and bedrock is called a soil profile.

Geotechnical engineers worked on a flood protection project in Toronto, Canada. The team used solutions such as building up the land beside the Don River to prevent overflow from reaching the floodplain.

FLOODPLAINS

Erosion beside rivers and streams can create **floodplains**. The flow of river water carries away sediment, which lowers the ground level and makes it more likely to flood. Geotechnical engineers design foundations that are stable in flooded soil. They also design drains that help prevent flooding by allowing excess water to leave the soil. Another option is building flood protection such as embankments. These rock and soil walls prevent waterways from overflowing. Sometimes engineers identify floodplains that should not be developed because the risk of damage is simply too high.

Investigating soil

Geotechnical engineers examine the subsoil at the beginning of a design project because it affects the foundation of a structure. They can tell how soil will move under pressure or when it is on an angle, called a slope. They must understand how the soil will absorb water such as rain. Their investigations also help construction teams plan safe **excavation**. Sandy soil drains and compacts well because of the size and shape of its grains. It is ideal for construction sites. Clay expands as it absorbs water, then shrinks as it dries. Structures on clay soil may move or crack. However, clay mixed with silt expands less, so it works well as a base. Engineers may suggest ways to improve poor soil. Builders can remove and replace soil, or add materials to improve it.

FORCES AND STRESSES

Geotechnical engineers understand how Earth's crust reacts to **forces** that push and pull it. Heat energy created inside the planet slowly moves massive pieces of Earth's crust and upper mantle, called tectonic plates, over the lower mantle. Forces including Earth's gravity and the force created by Earth's rotation place **stress** on rocks and cause them to shift and strain. Rock may change size, form, or volume. Three major types of stress affect rocks. Tensional stress occurs when forces pull rocks in opposite directions. Shear stress happens when rocks slide against each other as they move in opposite directions. Compressional stress occurs when rocks are pushed together. To avoid excavation and building problems, geotechnical engineers look for forces and stresses that affect the underlying bedrock.

MODELING STRESS

Your hands will provide the force in this activity. However, you probably can't break a rock just using your hands. Instead, use a large, soft bar of modeling clay to model rock stress.

Tensional stress: Using both hands, hold the bar of modeling clay at each end, and pull it apart into two pieces.

Shear stress: Press the flat sides of two pieces of modeling back together. While still pressing them together, push upward on one piece and downward on the other. How does the modeling clay look now?

Compressional stress: Put one piece of modeling clay between your hands. Push your hands together using as much strength as possible. Notice how the crushed clay changed shape. Did you use enough force to create peaks in the clay?

Tensional stress
A fracture in Earth's crust, called a fault, forms when rocks under tensional stress are pulled apart. When two separate faults form, the ground between them is pushed down or up.

Shear stress
Shear stress caused by tectonic plates scraping against each other created this crack, known as the San Andreas Fault, in California.

Compressional stress
The Himalaya mountains in Asia are rising by about 0.2 inches (5 mm) each year because of the compressional stress caused by tectonic plates pushing together underneath it.

NATURAL HAZARDS

One of the roles of geotechnical engineers is to consider the impact of natural hazards on a project. No one can prevent natural hazards such as volcanic eruptions and **tsunamis**. However, geotechnical engineers can tell where they might occur. Engineers learn from past catastrophic events. They find patterns in the locations, timing, and power of these events. They use this data to avoid the collapse of unstable structures during disasters. Engineers decide which sites are too risky for development because the potential for natural hazards is too high. In safer areas, they design foundations and supports that minimize the effects of hazards. They also help teams that upgrade structures to prevent problems. This process adds new parts to existing structures to make them stronger.

The blue lines on the map below show the boundaries between tectonic plates.

TECTONIC PLATES

Mapping is an important tool that geotechnical engineers use to keep people safe from possible disasters. The locations of natural hazards such as earthquakes and volcanoes are not random. Most of them are on the boundaries between tectonic plates. Maps such as this one show tectonic plate boundaries.

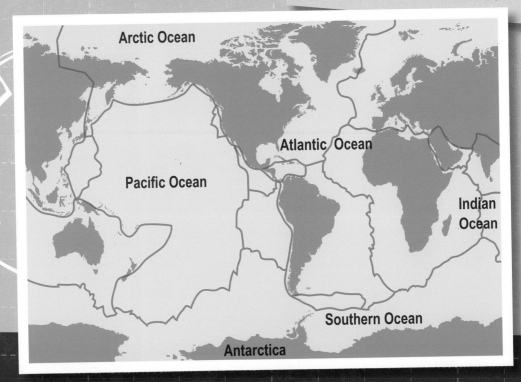

An earthquake rocked Christchurch, New Zealand, on February 22, 2011. It only lasted 10 seconds, but it caused widespread damage.

CAUSES OF NATURAL HAZARDS

Stresses caused by weathering, erosion, and the movement of tectonic plates can lead to natural hazards. Most earthquakes happen when rocks under stress at tectonic plate boundaries move suddenly. Huge tsunami waves can form when an earthquake occurs in Earth's crust under the ocean. Volcanic eruptions occur when magma rises up from Earth's mantle and bursts through tectonic plates or along fault lines. Earthquakes, volcanic eruptions, and unstable slopes can cause landslides, including mudslides and rockslides. Sinkholes occur when subsoil and bedrock are washed away underground and the ground above them collapses. Sinkholes form in many ways, but erosion is one of the main causes. Land sinks because of human activity, too. When we pump our water supply out of the ground, it can weaken the soil. Severe weather such as hurricanes and tornadoes are also natural hazards. Geotechnical engineers must consider all these potential natural hazards when they plan and design projects.

Vancouver, Canada, has a high risk of earthquake activity. Geotechnical engineers helped upgrade Vancouver's Lions Gate Bridge. Vancouver lies in the most earthquake-prone part of Canada.

BUILDING ON THE PAST

Like today's societies, ancient civilizations used Earth's materials for impressive construction projects. In what is now Iraq, the ancient Mesopotamians, for example, built dams on rivers to collect water in **reservoirs**. Waterways were dug to bring water to crops. They made embankments to prevent flooding. Mixtures of soils were compacted and cemented together with water to create foundations. Ancient builders used experience as their guide. If something worked well in the past, they kept doing it. If a design failed, they tried something different the next time.

LEANING TOWER OF PISA

In 1173, construction began on a cathedral bell tower in Pisa, Italy. The builders were not aware that setting the shallow foundation in loose silt with water levels that changed during the rainy seasons would lead to problems. The ground beneath the structure began to sink within a few years because of a process known as **subsidence**. The tower became known as the Leaning Tower of Pisa. All attempts to straighten it failed. Over the centuries, people searched for solutions to this challenge and others like it. A geotechnical engineer from England finally solved how to stabilize the tower in 2001. John Burland's idea was to remove small amounts of soil from beneath one side of the tower. Gravity helped force the Leaning Tower of Pisa upright. A couple of years later, Burland added a drainage system that keeps the changing water levels in the soil from affecting the tower's foundations.

The Leaning Tower of Pisa was just one of the sinking foundations that led to the first scientific theories about soil in the 1700s.

Built to last

Some ancient foundations were so well built that the structures they support still stand today. The pyramids in Egypt were an amazing design challenge. Built between 2700 and 1800 BCE, some pyramids included complex foundations and underground construction. We do not know much about the ancient Egyptians' design processes, but some people believe they learned the importance of site locations and stable slopes through hundreds of years of trial and error. More than 1,000 years later, the ancient Greeks understood even more about stable foundations. In Athens, they built shallow stone foundations on sturdy ground.

The Parthenon, a temple in Athens, Greece, has stood for almost 2,500 years!

ST. FRANCIS DAM COLLAPSE

When California's St. Francis Dam collapsed in 1928, about 500 people living downstream died in the resulting flood. The dam was brand new—construction finished less than two years before it failed. There was a hurried investigation that left unanswered questions about the cause of the collapse. Many theories have been put forward over the years. Experts ruled out the possibility of an earthquake. One side of the dam rested on what may have been an old landslide. This ground may have been unstable. Parts of the foundation were thin, weak layers of metamorphic rock. The layers broke under the force of the water stored in the reservoir on one side of the dam. In addition, erosion carried away soil at the dam's base. This may have caused shifting in the foundation. After this disaster, the need for study in the new field of geotechnical engineering was clear.

The St. Francis Dam collapse was one of the worst engineering disasters in the past century.

MODERN GEOTECHNICAL ENGINEERS

Geotechnical engineers use science, math, and computers to solve design challenges related to Earth's materials and processes. They also need plenty of creative ideas. Their scientific knowledge and engineering skills are useful for many kinds of projects. Geotechnical engineers consult with **civil engineers** who plan cities and urban areas. They recommend safe building locations and create suitable foundation

Geotechnical engineers work in offices, onsite at construction projects, and in labs.

designs. They also suggest ways to protect rocks and soil in developed areas. Places that are likely to face natural hazards need geotechnical engineers. Some local governments require reports by geotechnical engineers before building can begin. Their expertise is also useful for oil and mining operations that remove minerals, rocks, and other resources from the ground.

Communication and teamwork: Geotechnical engineers must be able to explain their data and solutions clearly. They collaborate, or work together with other engineers, such as structural or materials engineers. They work with scientists, architects, builders, and property owners, too. A group of people that includes professionals from more than one field is called an interdisciplinary team. Geotechnical engineers commonly share their expertise on interdisciplinary teams. Senior geotechnical engineers may manage teams as well.

THE CHANNEL TUNNEL

An interdisciplinary team of engineers, scientists, designers, and builders worked together on the Channel Tunnel that connects England to France. Train tracks in two separate tunnels were constructed about 150 feet (46 m) below the seabed, or floor, of the English Channel. Geotechnical engineers profiled the rock and soil long before construction began in 1987. They helped find the ideal depth to dig, where there was chalky clay that would keep out excess water. They ruled out a possible disaster due to tectonic plate movements. One of their important findings was that the sedimentary rock on the French side of the Channel contained more stress fractures than the rock on the English side. Using this data, other engineers designed tunneling machines that would work in the different rock and soil conditions. When tunneling began, British geotechnical engineer Helen Nattrass and her team led the way. They confirmed that the rock and soil conditions were as earlier studies predicted. Their efforts made it safe for people to work in the tunnels. Geotechnical engineers also checked that the soil interacted with the new concrete tunnels as expected.

The American Society of Civil Engineers called the Channel Tunnel one of the seven wonders of the modern world.

STARTING THE PROCESS

Geotechnical engineers may work on each step of the design process. They often assist other engineers and designers with some stages but not the whole process. Geotechnical engineers were part of an interdisciplinary team working on a project in Venice, Italy. The design process began by clearly identifying a complex problem that the city faced.

Defining the problem: A team of experts, including geotechnical engineers, took on the challenge of solving how to stop flooding in Venice. The city spreads over more than 100 islands. They are in a **coastal lagoon** that connects to the Adriatic Sea. Water surrounds the structures where people live and work. Two main factors put them in danger: land sinking because of subsidence and rising sea levels. The ground has lowered slowly over the centuries since the historic city's founding. To reduce subsidence in the 1970s, Venice closed nearly 20,000 wells that drew water out of the ground. However, the land continues to sink because of moving tectonic plates and soil compacting under the weight of buildings. Venice subsides, or sinks, by about 0.08 inches (2 mm) each year. The additional problem of rising sea levels is caused by the rise in Earth's temperatures, called global warming. There is also a link between climate change and increasingly extreme storms that lead to flooding.

The problem of flooding in Venice first received serious attention after a major flood in 1966.

Determining details

After defining the problem, geotechnical engineers work out the details of the task. Before they consider solutions, they identify the criteria, or needs, of the project. They ask what the solution must achieve to be successful. They also look at the constraints of the design. Constraints are the limits, such as cost, time, or location, that must be considered when looking for a solution.

*Hundreds of bridges join Venice's islands. The Rialto Bridge was built in 1591, long before geotechnical engineering existed. Its foundation uses over 10,000 **piles** made of tree trunks, which were driven into the clay subsoil.*

Identifying criteria and constraints: After defining and researching the problem, the team considered the project's criteria and constraints. The final design or system needed to keep people safe. It also needed to prevent flood damage to historically important buildings. The solution had to protect the whole lagoon and work for many years. Constraints included the fact that much of Venice is under water, which makes construction more challenging. Although the Italian government planned to spend billions of dollars on the project, the budget would limit some design ideas. There were also environmental concerns. The design had to do as little harm as possible to the local wildlife.

SEARCHING FOR SOLUTIONS

After geotechnical engineers identify a problem and work out the project's criteria and constraints, they brainstorm solutions. They may work alone or collaborate with a team. They come up with as many ideas as possible that could potentially solve the problem. Even suggestions that seem strange go on the list. Later in the brainstorming stage, engineers research the ideas that seem most likely to work.

Brainstorming ideas: Some people on the Venice flood-prevention team suggested pumping water back into the city's ground to raise it. Other ideas included reducing erosion on shorelines or improving the soil to make it resistant to flooding. Possible solutions came from other countries as well. Netherlands had the largest flood protection system in the world. It used dams and barriers to keep high tides from swamping coastal areas. London, England, is protected from flooding by moveable gates in the Thames Barrier. Could Venice construct something similar to protect it from the Adriatic Sea?

When experts from different fields brainstorm together, they can think of many innovative solutions.

Systems such as the Thames Barrier provided inspiration for the solution to flooding in Venice. The gates on the Thames lie flat on the seabed until high tides are forecast. Then they rotate and rise to protect the floodplains around the city of London.

Selecting an approach

The most promising ideas are those that seem to meet the project criteria and constraints. Geotechnical engineers and their collaborators decide which design or approach is most likely to solve the problem. This potential solution is the one they will develop. They also consider trade-offs, when one or more important details are set aside so that other key criteria or constraints can be met.

Choosing a design: After considering all the pros and cons of the most workable ideas, the Venice team decided to develop flood barriers. Data collected by geotechnical engineers helped the team select an approach. Geotechnical engineers had identified that the soil was mainly silt, and that a mixture of sediments covered the seabed. They had also studied processes such as erosion and the movement of tectonic plates. They agreed that flood barriers could be anchored securely and safely to Venice's seabed. In addition to helping with the main flood-barrier project, geotechnical engineers would also assist with projects aimed at reducing erosion and making the soil less prone to subsidence.

A trade-off in using the barriers was the possible environmental damage the structures could cause. Marine animals and plants living in the lagoon might be disturbed by the barriers. However, people from many different areas of expertise decided it was more important to save the city from flooding.

Working on seabeds is nothing new for geotechnical engineers. Their site investigations and design ideas are used in the construction of offshore oil rigs and structures like these wind turbines.

PROTOTYPE TESTING CYCLE

Engineers build models called **prototypes** to try out their ideas. They test and redesign them in a repeating series of steps called a cycle. Design improvements and trade-offs are made. In some cases, engineers might realize that their approach does not solve the problem. If that happens, they select another possible solution and a new cycle begins. In Venice, the prototype testing cycle took several years. MOSE was the short-form name for the full-size model. Soon people started calling the whole project MOSE.

Constructing a prototype:

Engineers build prototypes to test their proposed solutions. First, engineers sketch details of their designs. They may also create computer models. Then they build physical prototypes. The Venice project team constructed a variety of computer and **scale models** before making a full-size prototype. Geotechnical engineers collaborated with other engineers during prototyping. They designed concrete foundations called caissons. These watertight bases would be stable and strong on the seabed.

A frame built around the full-size MOSE prototype included all the equipment needed to test it.

Testing and assessing

Prototypes are tested in **computer simulations**, labs, and in the environments where the designs will be used. The MOSE team also used scale models of Venice and its lagoon to see how their solution would perform. Then they installed a full-size prototype in Venice's lagoon. They were not testing how well it held back high tides. One gate could not do that alone. Instead, the prototype's materials, technologies, and structure were studied. Geotechnical engineers studied how the soil settled beneath the prototype. They wanted to ensure that the soil compacted evenly, so the foundation was stable.

The MOSE team used a 129,000-square-foot (12,000 m²) model of Venice to test their ideas. It allowed them to simulate the effects of high tides.

Refining the design

No one expects the first prototype to be free of flaws. Engineers suggest ideas for redesign after they identify problems. The MOSE team had many experts improving different parts of the design. For example, geotechnical engineers looked at how sediment collected on top of the barriers when they laid flat on the seabed. Adding a way to remove the sediment was just one potential revision. The whole team learned from the successes and failures of the full-size prototype. Over years of testing, it was removed from the lagoon for design changes. Then the prototype was returned to the water for more testing. Finally, the MOSE flood barrier design was ready to go into production.

SHARING THE RESULTS

When geotechnical engineers are ready to share their designs, they rely on their communications skills. They might explain their design processes at conferences, where people with common interests meet. Sometimes the public is interested in learning about the process, too. Geotechnical engineers may also write articles for engineering and scientific **journals**. In addition, they must clearly communicate their designs to the people who will build them.

Telling the story: After the MOSE prototype was refined, the team was ready to share their solution. Before the barriers could be put in place across the lagoon, their results had to be presented to various levels of the Italian government for approval. Geotechnical engineers on the team explained their site investigations and their parts in the design process. The project was a major news story around the world. Many people were interested in the design process and results. Not everyone agreed about the trade-off that ranked people and buildings over local wildlife. The team had to defend why they designed a solution that could cause different problems for the environment.

The decision about when to activate the MOSE flood barriers is made by human operators. **Compressed air** flows into the hinged gates, which float upward. When they are raised, the barriers stop high tides from reaching Venice. When the air is released, water enters the gates. They sink and lie flat on the seabed.

PREVENTING DISASTERS

Like Venice, New Orleans in Louisiana is in a high-risk area for flooding. Lakes, canals, and the Mississippi River surround the area. Flood barriers called levees were built to protect the city. However, over 50 of these levees failed during Hurricane Katrina in 2005. The sandy subsoil swelled with water and became unstable. This probably caused the bases of some levees to shift and weaken. Many barriers collapsed under the weight of the floodwaters. Poor levee designs and construction were among the main reasons for the disaster. It highlighted the need for geotechnical engineering and a thorough design process. Before the U.S. Army Corps of Engineers built a new system to prevent flooding, they ran more than 60,000 computer simulations of their designs. The new system also accounted for soil subsidence and global warming. People involved in flood prevention around the world watched as the Army Corps engineers attempted to prevent another disaster. The engineers shared their solutions, which could help other places avoid major flood damage.

Construction crews build the designs created by engineers.
These workers are finishing new levees in New Orleans.

DESIGN CHALLENGE

Are you ready to try out your engineering skills? Follow the design process to create a strong foundation. You will need the following materials:

- package of drinking straws (or similarly shaped materials, such as pencils)

- modeling clay

- a shallow tray (a dish or a box will also work)

- enough sand and marbles to fill the tray

Pour a layer of marbles into the tray. Then pour a layer of sand over the marbles. These materials represent weak and shifting rocks and soil. The tray beneath them is the firm bedrock. Your foundation building materials are the clay and straws. Your goal is to ensure that the foundation and the structure it supports do not shift when you move the tray.

One World Trade Center was built with a very strong foundation. Steel beams and 40 truckloads of concrete anchored the building directly to the metamorphic bedrock.

1: Define the problem: Clearly describe your challenge. If you are working with a friend, compare how you each define the problem. Your goal is to design a strong foundation that will support a structure.

2: Investigate the problem: Consider your criteria and constraints. Your foundation needs to be stable even in shifting marbles and sand. Your solution might succeed if it involves a way to attach the foundation and structure firmly. You are limited by the amount and strength of your building materials. Another constraint is the size of your site (tray).

3: Brainstorm: It's time to come up with ideas for strong foundation designs. Also, consider if there are ways you could improve the ground (sand and marbles). Which ideas do you think are the most likely to work? Develop those ideas. Draw or describe as many details as possible.

4: Select a design: Review your criteria and constraints. Which of your potential solutions do you think will meet them? What are the pros and cons of each idea? Choose the design that you think is the best idea to develop.

5: Build a prototype: Sketch a complete diagram and figure out all the design details before constructing a prototype foundation. You should expect some flaws in the first version of your prototype—that's normal.

6: Test the model: It's time to test your prototype. Gently move the tray so that the marbles and sand shift. Does your foundation or structure shift? Repeat the tests to check your results.

7: Improve the design: Consider your test results. What worked well—or not so well? List any changes you need to make to your design. Does the foundation need to be larger or deeper? Is it firmly attached to the bedrock (tray)? Should you compact the sand into the marbles? Would increasing the water content in your sand help it cement together?

8: Communicate the solution: Record your process and results. To practice your skills as an engineer, include diagrams and clear instructions that will help you or anyone else recreate the design. Present your findings to a friend or family member.

INTO THE FUTURE

Earth's materials will not change much in your lifetime. However, the ways that geotechnical engineers work with them might change. Engineers will always be searching for new solutions to new problems. One future challenge is aging urban systems. Some cities were built before geotechnical engineering was widespread. Geotechnical engineers will work with civil engineers on innovative ways to update older foundations. For example, they could reinforce weathered foundations with steel or concrete. Another future concern is **sustainability** for large cities. Geotechnical engineers can suggest how to use natural resources such as the water stored in rocks and soil. With the rise in the world's population, more land will be needed for people to live on. Some of this land may have poor rock and soil conditions, or be in natural hazard zones. Engineers need to meet these challenges and design safe structures.

NEW TECHNOLOGIES AND MATERIALS

Advances in technologies and materials will change geotechnical engineering in the future. More powerful computers will help engineers create and test designs. For example, simulations of the impacts of natural hazards on solutions such as flood barriers may be made even more accurate. Improved robotics and machinery will help with the collection and testing of rock and soil samples. New, stronger concretes will make stronger foundations. The use of **geosynthetic** materials is also on the rise with engineering projects. These ground-improving products include fabrics, plastics, and foam. Geosynthetics can be laid on top of the ground or be placed between layers of soil or rocks. They have many uses, including supporting Earth's materials so they do not erode. They also help keep pollutants out of the soils at landfill sites.

Geosynthetics line some modern landfills and prevent waste from seeping into the soil.

The Burj Khalifa skyscraper was built on an unusual triangular foundation.

It is 2,722 feet (830 m) tall. That means it stands over half a mile (0.8 km) above the ground! The building's foundation must support massive loads.

STANDING TALL

There will always be competition to build the world's tallest structure. These skyscrapers place huge amounts of weight on the soil and rocks beneath them. Geotechnical engineers help find locations where the soil is suitable and away from natural hazards. They also work with other civil engineers to design foundations that can hold the loads. The Burj Khalifa in Dubai, United Arab Emirates, became the tallest building on Earth when it was completed in 2010. The geotechnical site investigation found that sandy soil covered weak sedimentary rock. To keep the building from sinking, 192 steel piles were driven more than 160 feet (49 m) underground! They hold up a huge slab of concrete, called a raft foundation. Designers are already coming up with solutions for structures that will top the Burj Khalifa!

LEARNING MORE

BOOKS

Cook, Eric. *Prototyping.* Cherry Lake Publishing, 2015.

Aloian, Molly. *Different Kinds of Soil.* Crabtree Publishing, 2010.

Gray, Susan Heinrichs. *Geology: The Study of Rocks.* Scholastic, 2012.

Greve, Tom. *Plate Tectonics and Disasters.* Rourke Publishing Group, 2012.

Hyde, Natalie. *What Is the Rock Cycle?* Crabtree Publishing, 2011.

Hyde, Natalie. *Soil Erosion and How to Prevent It.* Crabtree Publishing, 2010.

ONLINE

www.whatisgeotech.org

Check out real-life examples of what geotechnical engineers do.

www.cotf.edu/ete/modules/msese/ earthsys.html

Learn more about the rock cycle and plate tectonics on the Earth Science Explorer site.

www.soils4kids.org

Dig deeper! This site has plenty of fun soil facts and activities.

http://science.nationalgeographic.com/ science/earth/the-dynamic-earth/

Find out about Earth's processes on the Dynamic Earth section of National Geographic's website.

www.esa.int/esaKIDSen/ Naturaldisasters.html

The European Space Agency's site has pages dedicated to a variety of natural hazards.

GLOSSARY

acid rain Precipitation containing acidic chemicals caused by pollution

civil engineer A type of engineer who works with structures such as buildings, dams, and bridges—geotechnical engineers are civil engineers

clay Fine, stiff soil that changes texture depending on whether it is wet or dry

coastal lagoon A shallow body of water beside a shore that is naturally separated, in part or completely, from the open ocean

compressed air Air that is under greater pressure than that of Earth's atmosphere

computer simulation A computer model that acts in a similar way to an actual object

core sample A cylinder of material that is drawn from the ground using a special hollow drill

decomposed Decayed or rotted

erosion A process by which material is worn away from Earth's surface

excavation Digging in the ground

floodplain A strip of flat and normally dry land alongside a stream, river, or lake that becomes covered by water during a flood

force The push or pull needed to move things or change their shape

foundation The supportive base of a structure, which is usually underground

geosynthetic Geosynthetics are artificial (human-made) materials used to stabilize an area of ground

igneous Describing rock that is composed of solidified magma

journal A magazine focused on a special topic

landfill A site where layers of waste are covered by layers of soil

magma Hot, liquid material that forms beneath Earth's crust

metamorphic Describing rock that has been transformed from igneous or sedimentary rock by pressure and heat

minerals Solid materials that form naturally and are the main ingredients of rock and soil

pile A post that is driven into the ground to secure a foundation

prototype A model of a design built for testing

reservoir A water supply, usually stored in a large lake

scale model A physical copy that has the same proportions as an actual object, but might be a different size

sediment Small pieces of Earth's materials that are moved by erosion

sedimentary Describing rock that is formed by cemented and compacted sediment

silt Very fine soil composed of sediment

soil mechanics The study of soil properties and behavior

stress Tension or pressure that is applied to an object

subsidence The sinking or caving in of land caused by movements below Earth's surface

sustainability The ability to use natural resources while also protecting them for future use

tsunami A very large ocean wave caused by natural hazards such as an earthquake under the ocean

INDEX

bedrock 6, 10, 13, 26, 27
brainstorming 5, 20, 27
bridges 4, 13, 19
Burj Khalifa 29

clay 8, 9, 17, 19
computers 16, 22, 23, 28
conferences 24
core samples 6
crust 6, 10, 13

dams 14, 15, 20
design process 5, 6, 15, 18–25, 26–27

earthquakes 12, 13, 15
environment 4, 19, 21, 24
erosion 8, 9, 13, 15, 20, 21, 28

flood protection 9, 14, 18–25, 28
floodplains 9, 20
foundations 4, 5, 6, 9, 12, 14, 15, 16, 19, 22, 23, 26, 27, 28, 29
future designs 28–29

geosynthetics 28

igneous rocks 7

landfills 4, 28
landslides 13, 15
Leaning Tower of Pisa 14
levees 25

magma 6, 7, 13
mantle 6, 10, 13
metamorphic rocks 7, 15, 26

One World Trade Center 26

piles 19, 29
prototypes 5, 22–23, 24, 27

rock cycle 6, 7

sand 6, 8, 9, 25, 26, 26, 27, 29
scientists 4, 16, 17
sediment 7, 8, 9, 21, 23
sedimentary rocks 7, 17, 29
silt 8, 9, 14, 21
skyscrapers 4, 29
stresses 10, 11, 13, 17
subsidence 14, 18, 21, 25
subsoil 8, 9, 13, 19, 25

tectonic plates 10, 11, 12, 13, 17, 18, 21
testing 5, 6, 22–23, 27, 28
topsoil 8
trade-offs 21, 22, 24
tsunamis 12, 13
tunnels 4, 17

volcanoes 12, 13
Von Terzaghi, Karl 5

weathering 8, 13